CW00430222

## How you can help

Help your child to develop reading and language skills by looking through the book together. Look closely at the pictures and talk about what you see. Your child will soon learn to recognise the images and enjoy matching the words to the pictures.

## Contents




Cover photograph by Garie Hind

A catalogue record for this book is available from the British Library

Published by Ladybird Books Ltd
80 Strand London WC2R 0RL
A Penguin Company

4 6 8 10 9 7 5 3

first steps with ladybird

# 100 verbs

by Viv Lambert
illustrated by Andrew Everitt-Stewart

# In the morning

Wake up.

Get up.

Brush my teeth.

Comb my hair.

Smile in the mirror.

Wash my face.

Get dressed.

Drink juice.

Eat breakfast.

# At home

Make a cake. Turn on the computer.

Have my lunch. Sweep the floor.

Watch TV.

Tidy my room.

Cook some food.

Clean the windows.

# At school

Spell my name.

Take an apple.

Write a story.

Paint a picture.

Count the pencils.

Clap my hands.

Cut out my picture.

Draw a square.

Colour the animals.

# With my friends

Sing a song.

Talk to friends.

Pretend to be
a princess.

Hide behind a tree.

Hold hands.

Share a snack.

Whisper a secret.

Laugh at a joke.

# At the weekend

Listen to music.

Dance at the party.

Look at the animals.

Play the piano.

Wear my trainers.

Play football.

Skate in the park.

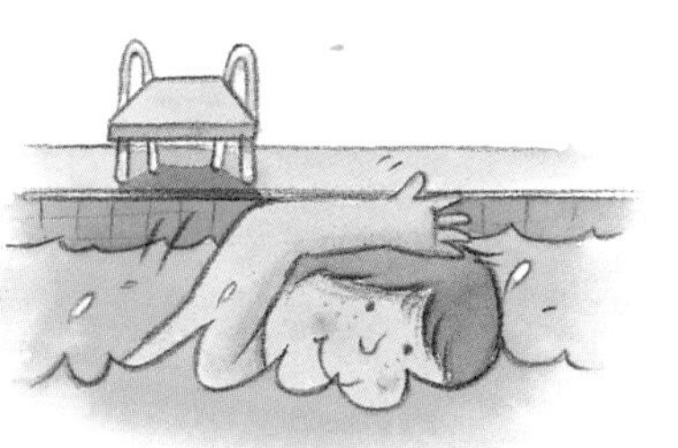

Give a present.

Swim in the pool.

# In the park

Ride a bike.

Fly a kite.

Run round the track.

Skip with a rope.

Sail a boat.

See my friends.

Kick a ball.

Walk the dog.

# In the garden

Throw a ball.

Catch a ball.

Pick a flower.

Climb a tree.

Plant some seeds.

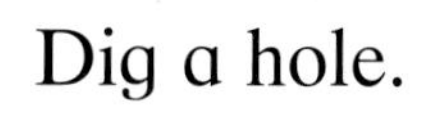

Dig a hole.

Jump in the sand.

Water the flowers.

# Children

Fall over.

Cry for Mummy.

Learn a game.

Lose the ball.

Find a shell.

Fight over toys.

Stand up.

Sit down.

# Grown ups

Phone someone.

Work hard.

Look after me.

Shout sometimes.

Love me.

Go out.

Give me presents.

Help me.

# In town

Wait for the bus.

Stop the bus.

Get on the bus.

Get off the bus.

Meet a friend.

Drive a car.

Build a road.

Shop for clothes.

# Going shopping

Smell fresh bread.

Taste some cheese.

Choose a cake.

Carry a bag.

Sell magazines.

Push a trolley.

Pay the shopkeeper.

Weigh some fruit.

Buy a comic.

# Bedtime

Have a bath.

Go to bed.

Read a story.

Switch off the light.

Hug my teddy.

Kiss Daddy.

Sleep all night.

Dream sweet dreams.